W9-BRT-049

COWS ON THE FARM/
VACAS DE GRANJA

By Rose Carraway

Traducción al español: Eduardo Alamán

Gareth Stevens
Publishing

Please visit our website, www.garethstevens.com. For a free color catalog of all our high-quality books, call toll free 1-800-542-2595 or fax 1-877-542-2596.

Library of Congress Cataloging-in-Publication Data

Carraway, Rose.
[Cows on the farm. English & Spanish]
Cows on the farm = Vacas de granja / Rose Carraway.
    p. cm. — (Farm animals = Animales de granja)
Includes index.
ISBN 978-1-4339-7396-3 (library binding)
1. Dairy cattle—Juvenile literature. I. Title. II. Title: Vacas de granja.
SF208.C3718 2013
636.2′142—dc23

2011052949

First Edition

Published in 2013 by
Gareth Stevens Publishing
111 East 14th Street, Suite 349
New York, NY 10003

Copyright © 2013 Gareth Stevens Publishing

Editor: Katie Kawa
Designer: Andrea Davison-Bartolotta
Spanish Translation: Eduardo Alamán

Photo credits: Cover, p. 1 Pixel Memoirs/Shutterstock.com; pp. 5, 17, 19, 24 (barn, switch) iStockphoto/Thinkstock; p. 7 tepic/Shutterstock.com; p. 9 basketman23/Shutterstock.com; p. 11 (main) Wally Stemberger/Shutterstock.com; p. 11 (inset) Adriana Nikolova/Shutterstock.com; p. 13 Dave McAleavy/Shutterstock.com; p. 15 Phillip W. Kirkland/Shutterstock.com; pp. 21, 24 (hay) iStockphoto.com/Nicky Gordon; p. 23 F1online/Thinkstock.

Printed in the United States of America

CPSIA compliance information: Batch #CS12GS: For further information contact Gareth Stevens, New York, New York at 1-800-542-2595.

Contents

Dairy Cows 4

A Cow's Tail 16

Life in the Herd 20

Words to Know 24

Index 24

Contenido

Vacas lecheras. .4

La cola de las vacas 16

Vida en la manada 20

Palabras que debes saber 24

Índice 24

Cows live in a barn.

Las vacas viven en establos.

One kind of cow is a dairy cow. Farmers get milk from dairy cows.

Un tipo de vaca es la vaca lechera. Estas vacas le dan leche a los granjeros.

Some farmers use their hands to milk cows. Some use machines.

Algunos granjeros usan sus manos para ordeñar las vacas. Otros usan máquinas.

9

Milk from cows makes
ice cream!

¡La leche de las
vacas se usa para
hacer helado!

Many dairy cows
have spots.
The spots are black.

Muchas vacas lecheras
tienen manchas. Las
manchas son de
color negro.

A baby cow is called
a calf.

El bebé de la vaca se
llama becerro.

A cow has a long tail.
The end of the tail
is called the switch.

Las vacas tienen largas
colas. A estas colas se
les llama rabos.

17

It keeps flies away.

Con el rabo, las vacas
ahuyentan las moscas.

Cows eat grass
and hay.

Las vacas comen hierba
y heno.

Cows like to live in groups. A group of cows is called a herd.

A las vacas les gusta vivir en grupos. Un grupo de vacas se llama manada.

Words to Know/
Palabras que debes saber

barn/
(el) establo

hay/
(el) heno

switch/
(el) rabo

Index / Índice

calf/(el) becerro 14

herd/(la) manada 22

milk/(la) leche 6, 8, 10

switch/(el) rabo 16

24